50 French Soup Recipes for Home

By: Kelly Johnson

Table of Contents

- Soupe à l'Oignon (French Onion Soup)
- Vichyssoise
- Bouillabaisse
- Potage Parmentier (Leek and Potato Soup)
- Soupe au Pistou
- Soupe de Poissons (Fish Soup)
- Soupe à l'ail (Garlic Soup)
- Soupe à l'oignon gratinée (Gratinéed Onion Soup)
- Soupe de Haricots (Bean Soup)
- Soupe à l'oignon doux (Sweet Onion Soup)
- Soupe à la Provençale
- Soupe de Tomates à la Provençale (Provencal Tomato Soup)
- Soupe de Lentilles (Lentil Soup)
- Soupe à la Truffe (Truffle Soup)
- Soupe à l'oseille (Sorrel Soup)
- Soupe de Pois (Pea Soup)
- Soupe aux Champignons (Mushroom Soup)
- Soupe de Cresson (Watercress Soup)
- Soupe de Potiron (Pumpkin Soup)
- Soupe de Poisson à la Rouille (Fish Soup with Rouille)
- Soupe de Carottes (Carrot Soup)
- Soupe de Navet (Turnip Soup)
- Soupe à la Bière (Beer Soup)
- Soupe à la Fane de Radis (Radish Green Soup)
- Soupe aux Légumes (Vegetable Soup)
- Soupe aux Poireaux (Leek Soup)
- Soupe à la Châtaigne (Chestnut Soup)
- Soupe aux Moules (Mussel Soup)
- Soupe de Céleri-rave (Celery Root Soup)
- Soupe de Maïs (Corn Soup)
- Soupe aux Asperges (Asparagus Soup)
- Soupe au Cresson (Watercress Soup)
- Soupe au Vin Blanc (White Wine Soup)
- Soupe aux Poissons et aux Crustacés (Seafood Soup)
- Soupe de Patates Douces (Sweet Potato Soup)

- Soupe aux Choux (Cabbage Soup)
- Soupe aux Poireaux et Pommes de Terre (Potato Leek Soup)
- Soupe de Salsifis (Salsify Soup)
- Soupe au Pistou (Vegetable Soup with Pesto)
- Soupe de Champignons Sauvages (Wild Mushroom Soup)
- Soupe aux Fruits de Mer (Seafood Soup)
- Soupe aux Topinambours (Jerusalem Artichoke Soup)
- Soupe à l'Estragon (Tarragon Soup)
- Soupe de Poulet aux Vermicelles (Chicken Noodle Soup)
- Soupe à la Tomate (Tomato Soup)
- Soupe aux Légumes Verts (Green Vegetable Soup)
- Soupe de Poireaux et Pommes de Terre (Leek and Potato Soup)
- Soupe à l'Orange (Orange Soup)
- Soupe de Poireaux et Pommes de Terre (Leek and Potato Soup)
- Soupe à l'Estragon

Soupe à l'Oignon (French Onion Soup)

Ingredients:

- 4 large onions, thinly sliced
- 2 tablespoons butter
- 2 tablespoons olive oil
- 1 teaspoon sugar (optional, for caramelization)
- 4 cups beef broth
- 1 cup dry white wine
- Salt and pepper to taste
- Baguette slices, toasted
- Gruyère cheese, grated

Instructions:

1. Heat butter and olive oil in a large pot over medium heat. Add the sliced onions and cook, stirring occasionally, until they are caramelized and golden brown, about 30-40 minutes. Add sugar if using, to help with caramelization.
2. Deglaze the pot with white wine, scraping up any browned bits from the bottom. Cook for a few minutes until the wine has reduced slightly.
3. Pour in the beef broth and bring the soup to a simmer. Season with salt and pepper to taste. Allow to simmer for 15-20 minutes to blend the flavors.
4. Meanwhile, preheat your oven's broiler. Ladle the soup into oven-safe bowls. Top each bowl with a few slices of toasted baguette and sprinkle generously with grated Gruyère cheese.
5. Place the bowls under the broiler until the cheese is melted, bubbly, and golden brown, about 2-3 minutes.
6. Serve hot, being careful as the bowls will be hot from the broiler.

French Onion Soup is beloved for its savory broth, sweet caramelized onions, and gooey cheese topping. It's perfect for a comforting meal, especially during colder months.

Vichyssoise

Ingredients:

- 4 leeks, white and light green parts only, cleaned and sliced
- 2 tablespoons unsalted butter
- 2 medium potatoes, peeled and diced
- 4 cups chicken or vegetable broth
- 1 cup heavy cream
- Salt and white pepper, to taste
- Chives, finely chopped (for garnish, optional)

Instructions:

1. In a large pot, melt the butter over medium heat. Add the sliced leeks and cook until softened, about 5-7 minutes.
2. Add the diced potatoes and chicken or vegetable broth to the pot. Bring to a boil, then reduce the heat and simmer until the potatoes are tender, about 15-20 minutes.
3. Remove the pot from the heat and allow the soup to cool slightly.
4. Using an immersion blender or working in batches with a regular blender, puree the soup until smooth.
5. Stir in the heavy cream and season with salt and white pepper to taste. Chill the soup in the refrigerator for at least 2 hours or until completely cold.
6. Before serving, taste and adjust seasoning if needed. Serve the Vichyssoise chilled, garnished with chopped chives if desired.

Vichyssoise is a refreshing and elegant soup, perfect for summer or as a starter for a special meal. Its creamy texture and mild flavor make it a favorite among soup lovers.

Bouillabaisse

Ingredients:

- 1 lb mixed fish fillets (such as cod, haddock, snapper), cut into chunks
- 1 lb shellfish (such as shrimp, mussels, clams)
- 1 onion, chopped
- 2 cloves garlic, minced
- 1 fennel bulb, thinly sliced
- 1 leek, white and light green parts only, thinly sliced
- 1 tomato, chopped
- 1/2 cup white wine
- 4 cups fish or seafood broth
- 1/4 teaspoon saffron threads
- 1 bay leaf
- 1 tablespoon tomato paste
- Salt and pepper to taste
- Olive oil
- Rouille (a garlicky mayonnaise) and crusty bread for serving

Instructions:

1. In a large pot, heat olive oil over medium heat. Add the chopped onion, minced garlic, sliced fennel, and sliced leek. Cook until softened, about 5-7 minutes.
2. Stir in the chopped tomato and cook for another 2-3 minutes.
3. Add the white wine to the pot and let it simmer for a few minutes to reduce slightly.
4. Pour in the fish or seafood broth. Add the saffron threads, bay leaf, and tomato paste. Season with salt and pepper to taste. Bring the broth to a boil, then reduce the heat and let it simmer for about 20 minutes to develop flavors.
5. Add the mixed fish fillets to the pot and cook for 5-7 minutes, or until the fish is just cooked through.
6. Add the shellfish (shrimp, mussels, clams) to the pot and cook for another 5 minutes, or until the shells have opened (discard any unopened shells).
7. Taste the Bouillabaisse and adjust seasoning if needed. Remove the bay leaf before serving.
8. Serve the Bouillabaisse hot, accompanied with rouille and crusty bread on the side.

Bouillabaisse is a hearty and flavorful dish that showcases the bounty of the sea. It's perfect for a special occasion or a cozy dinner at home.

Potage Parmentier (Leek and Potato Soup)

Ingredients:

- 3 leeks, white and light green parts only, cleaned and thinly sliced
- 3 large potatoes, peeled and diced
- 1 onion, chopped
- 4 cups chicken or vegetable broth
- 1 cup milk or cream (optional, for creamier texture)
- 2 tablespoons unsalted butter
- Salt and pepper to taste
- Chives or parsley, finely chopped (for garnish, optional)

Instructions:

1. In a large pot, melt the butter over medium heat. Add the chopped onion and sliced leeks. Cook, stirring occasionally, until softened, about 5-7 minutes.
2. Add the diced potatoes to the pot and pour in the chicken or vegetable broth. Bring to a boil, then reduce the heat and simmer until the potatoes are tender, about 15-20 minutes.
3. Remove the pot from the heat and allow the soup to cool slightly.
4. Using an immersion blender or working in batches with a regular blender, puree the soup until smooth.
5. If using, stir in the milk or cream to achieve the desired consistency. Season with salt and pepper to taste.
6. Reheat the soup gently if needed. Serve hot, garnished with chopped chives or parsley if desired.

Potage Parmentier is a creamy and satisfying soup that highlights the sweetness of leeks and the earthiness of potatoes. It's perfect for a cozy meal, especially during colder weather.

Soupe au Pistou

Ingredients:

For the soup:

- 1 onion, chopped
- 2 cloves garlic, minced
- 2 carrots, diced
- 2 celery stalks, diced
- 1 zucchini, diced
- 1 potato, diced
- 1 cup green beans, chopped
- 1 can (14 oz) diced tomatoes
- 8 cups vegetable or chicken broth
- 1 cup small pasta (like ditalini or small shells)
- Salt and pepper to taste
- Olive oil

For the pistou:

- 2 cups fresh basil leaves, packed
- 2 cloves garlic, peeled
- 1/4 cup grated Parmesan cheese
- 1/4 cup olive oil
- Salt and pepper to taste

Instructions:

1. **Make the Soup:**
    - In a large pot, heat olive oil over medium heat. Add the chopped onion and minced garlic. Cook until softened, about 5 minutes.
    - Add the diced carrots, celery, zucchini, potato, and green beans to the pot. Cook for another 5 minutes, stirring occasionally.
    - Pour in the diced tomatoes and broth. Bring to a boil, then reduce the heat and let it simmer for about 20 minutes, or until the vegetables are tender.
    - Stir in the pasta and cook until al dente, following the package instructions.
    - Season with salt and pepper to taste. Keep warm while you prepare the pistou.
2. **Make the Pistou:**
    - In a food processor or blender, combine the basil leaves, garlic, and Parmesan cheese. Pulse until finely chopped.
    - With the motor running, slowly drizzle in the olive oil until the mixture is smooth and well combined.
    - Season with salt and pepper to taste.
3. **Serve:**
    - Ladle the hot soup into bowls. Spoon a generous dollop of pistou on top of each serving.
    - Serve immediately with crusty bread for a delicious and comforting meal.

Soupe au Pistou is a flavorful and vibrant soup that captures the essence of Provencal cuisine, with its fresh vegetables and aromatic basil-garlic sauce. It's perfect for enjoying during the summer months when vegetables are in season.

Soupe de Poissons (Fish Soup)

Ingredients:

For the soup base:

- 1 lb mixed fish fillets (such as cod, haddock, snapper), cut into chunks
- 1 lb mixed seafood (such as shrimp, mussels, clams)
- 1 onion, chopped
- 2 cloves garlic, minced
- 1 fennel bulb, thinly sliced
- 1 leek, white and light green parts only, thinly sliced
- 1 carrot, chopped
- 1 celery stalk, chopped
- 1 tomato, chopped
- 1/2 cup white wine
- 4 cups fish or seafood broth
- 1 bay leaf
- 1 teaspoon saffron threads
- 2 tablespoons tomato paste
- Salt and pepper to taste
- Olive oil

For the rouille:

- 1/2 cup mayonnaise
- 1-2 cloves garlic, minced
- 1 teaspoon paprika
- Dash of cayenne pepper (optional)

Instructions:

1. **Prepare the Soup Base:**
    - In a large pot, heat olive oil over medium heat. Add the chopped onion, minced garlic, sliced fennel, sliced leek, chopped carrot, and celery. Cook until softened, about 5-7 minutes.
    - Stir in the chopped tomato and cook for another 2-3 minutes.
    - Add the white wine to the pot and let it simmer for a few minutes to reduce slightly.
    - Pour in the fish or seafood broth. Add the bay leaf, saffron threads, and tomato paste. Season with salt and pepper to taste. Bring to a boil, then reduce the heat and let it simmer for about 20 minutes to develop flavors.
2. **Prepare the Rouille:**
    - In a small bowl, combine the mayonnaise, minced garlic, paprika, and cayenne pepper (if using). Mix well until smooth and set aside.
3. **Cook the Fish and Seafood:**
    - Add the mixed fish fillets to the pot and cook for 5-7 minutes, or until the fish is just cooked through.
    - Add the mixed seafood (shrimp, mussels, clams) to the pot and cook for another 5 minutes, or until the shells have opened (discard any unopened shells).

4. **Serve:**
    - Remove the bay leaf from the soup. Taste and adjust seasoning if needed.
    - Ladle the hot Fish Soup into bowls. Serve immediately with a dollop of rouille on top of each serving.
    - Serve with crusty bread for a complete and satisfying meal.

Soupe de Poissons is a delightful and robust soup that showcases the flavors of the sea. It's perfect for seafood lovers and makes for a memorable meal, especially when served with rouille and crusty bread.

Soupe à l'ail (Garlic Soup)

Ingredients:

- 1 head of garlic, about 10-12 cloves, peeled and thinly sliced
- 4 cups chicken or vegetable broth
- 1/2 cup dry white wine
- 2 tablespoons olive oil
- 2 slices of French bread, toasted and cut into cubes
- 1/2 cup grated Gruyère or Parmesan cheese
- Salt and pepper to taste
- Chopped parsley or chives for garnish (optional)

Instructions:

1. In a large pot, heat olive oil over medium heat. Add the thinly sliced garlic and sauté until fragrant and lightly golden, about 1-2 minutes.
2. Pour in the dry white wine and let it simmer for a few minutes to reduce slightly.
3. Add the chicken or vegetable broth to the pot. Bring to a boil, then reduce the heat and let it simmer for about 15-20 minutes to blend the flavors.
4. Season with salt and pepper to taste.
5. Ladle the hot soup into oven-safe bowls. Divide the toasted French bread cubes among the bowls, placing them on top of the soup.
6. Sprinkle grated Gruyère or Parmesan cheese over each bowl.
7. Place the bowls under a broiler for 2-3 minutes, or until the cheese is melted and bubbly.
8. Garnish with chopped parsley or chives if desired, and serve hot.

Soupe à l'ail is perfect for garlic lovers and makes a comforting meal, especially during colder months. The combination of garlic-infused broth, toasted bread, and melted cheese creates a satisfying and flavorful soup experience.

Soupe à l'oignon gratinée (Gratinéed Onion Soup)

Ingredients:

- 4 large onions, thinly sliced
- 2 tablespoons butter
- 2 tablespoons olive oil
- 1 teaspoon sugar (optional, for caramelization)
- 4 cups beef broth
- 1 cup dry white wine
- Salt and pepper to taste
- Baguette slices, toasted
- Gruyère cheese, grated

Instructions:

1. In a large pot, heat butter and olive oil over medium heat. Add the thinly sliced onions and cook, stirring occasionally, until they are caramelized and golden brown, about 30-40 minutes. Add sugar if using, to help with caramelization.
2. Deglaze the pot with white wine, scraping up any browned bits from the bottom. Cook for a few minutes until the wine has reduced slightly.
3. Pour in the beef broth and bring the soup to a simmer. Season with salt and pepper to taste. Allow to simmer for 15-20 minutes to blend the flavors.
4. Meanwhile, preheat your oven's broiler. Ladle the hot soup into oven-safe bowls.
5. Top each bowl with a few slices of toasted baguette.
6. Generously sprinkle grated Gruyère cheese over the bread slices and soup.
7. Place the bowls under the broiler until the cheese is melted, bubbly, and golden brown, about 2-3 minutes.
8. Carefully remove from the oven and serve hot.

Gratinéed Onion Soup is a comforting and flavorful dish, perfect for a cozy meal, especially during colder weather. The combination of sweet caramelized onions, savory broth, and melted cheese makes it a favorite among soup enthusiasts.

Soupe de Haricots (Bean Soup)

Ingredients:

- 1 cup dried white beans (such as navy beans or cannellini beans), soaked overnight and drained
- 1 onion, chopped
- 2 cloves garlic, minced
- 2 carrots, diced
- 2 celery stalks, diced
- 1 leek, white and light green parts only, thinly sliced
- 1 bay leaf
- 4 cups vegetable or chicken broth
- 1 tablespoon olive oil
- Salt and pepper to taste
- Chopped parsley or thyme for garnish (optional)

Instructions:

1. In a large pot, heat olive oil over medium heat. Add the chopped onion, minced garlic, diced carrots, diced celery, and sliced leek. Cook until softened, about 5-7 minutes.
2. Add the soaked and drained white beans to the pot. Pour in the vegetable or chicken broth.
3. Add the bay leaf to the pot. Bring to a boil, then reduce the heat to low. Cover and simmer for about 1 to 1.5 hours, or until the beans are tender. Stir occasionally and add more broth or water if needed to keep the beans covered.
4. Once the beans are tender, season the soup with salt and pepper to taste. Remove the bay leaf.
5. Using an immersion blender or working in batches with a regular blender, puree a portion of the soup to thicken it while leaving some beans whole for texture. Alternatively, you can mash some beans against the side of the pot with a spoon.
6. Serve hot, garnished with chopped parsley or thyme if desired.

This Bean Soup is nutritious and filling, perfect for a comforting meal, especially during colder months. It can be served as a starter or as a main dish with crusty bread on the side.

Soupe à l'oignon doux (Sweet Onion Soup)

Ingredients:

- 4 large sweet onions, thinly sliced
- 2 tablespoons butter
- 2 tablespoons olive oil
- 1 teaspoon sugar (optional, for caramelization)
- 4 cups beef or vegetable broth
- 1 cup dry white wine
- Salt and pepper to taste
- Baguette slices, toasted
- Gruyère or Swiss cheese, grated

Instructions:

1. In a large pot, heat butter and olive oil over medium heat. Add the thinly sliced sweet onions and cook, stirring occasionally, until they are caramelized and golden brown, about 30-40 minutes. Adding sugar during cooking can aid caramelization if desired.
2. Deglaze the pot with white wine, scraping up any browned bits from the bottom. Cook for a few minutes until the wine has reduced slightly.
3. Pour in the beef or vegetable broth and bring the soup to a simmer. Season with salt and pepper to taste. Allow to simmer for 15-20 minutes to blend the flavors.
4. Meanwhile, preheat your oven's broiler. Ladle the hot soup into oven-safe bowls.
5. Top each bowl with a few slices of toasted baguette.
6. Generously sprinkle grated Gruyère or Swiss cheese over the bread slices and soup.
7. Place the bowls under the broiler until the cheese is melted, bubbly, and golden brown, about 2-3 minutes.
8. Carefully remove from the oven and serve hot.

Sweet Onion Soup is a comforting and flavorful variation of French Onion Soup, perfect for those who enjoy milder, sweeter flavors. The combination of caramelized onions, savory broth, toasted bread, and melted cheese makes it a satisfying and warming dish, especially during cooler seasons.

Soupe à la Provençale

Ingredients:

- 2 tablespoons olive oil
- 1 onion, chopped
- 2 cloves garlic, minced
- 1 fennel bulb, thinly sliced
- 2 carrots, diced
- 2 celery stalks, diced
- 1 potato, peeled and diced
- 1 zucchini, diced
- 1 tomato, diced
- 1 can (14 oz) diced tomatoes
- 6 cups vegetable or chicken broth
- 1 bay leaf
- 1 teaspoon dried thyme
- Salt and pepper to taste
- 1 cup small pasta (such as ditalini or small shells)
- Fresh basil or parsley, chopped for garnish
- Grated Parmesan cheese for serving (optional)

Instructions:

1. In a large pot, heat olive oil over medium heat. Add the chopped onion and minced garlic. Cook until softened, about 5 minutes.
2. Add the thinly sliced fennel, diced carrots, diced celery, diced potato, and diced zucchini to the pot. Cook for another 5 minutes, stirring occasionally.
3. Stir in the diced tomato and canned diced tomatoes. Add the vegetable or chicken broth, bay leaf, and dried thyme. Season with salt and pepper to taste. Bring to a boil, then reduce the heat and let it simmer for about 20 minutes, or until the vegetables are tender.
4. Add the small pasta to the pot and cook until al dente, following the package instructions.
5. Taste and adjust seasoning if needed. Remove the bay leaf before serving.
6. Ladle the hot Provencal Soup into bowls. Garnish with chopped fresh basil or parsley.
7. Serve hot, optionally topping each serving with grated Parmesan cheese.

Provencal Soup is a vibrant and wholesome dish that showcases the flavors of fresh vegetables and aromatic herbs typical of Provence. It's perfect for a comforting meal, especially when served with crusty bread or a side salad.

Soupe de Tomates à la Provençale (Provencal Tomato Soup)

Ingredients:

- 2 tablespoons olive oil
- 1 onion, chopped
- 2 cloves garlic, minced
- 4-5 large tomatoes, chopped (about 4 cups)
- 1 can (14 oz) diced tomatoes
- 1 tablespoon tomato paste
- 4 cups vegetable or chicken broth
- 1 bay leaf
- 1 teaspoon dried thyme
- 1 teaspoon dried basil
- Salt and pepper to taste
- 1/2 cup heavy cream (optional, for a creamier soup)
- Fresh basil or parsley, chopped for garnish
- Croutons for serving (optional)

Instructions:

1. In a large pot, heat olive oil over medium heat. Add the chopped onion and minced garlic. Cook until softened, about 5 minutes.
2. Add the chopped fresh tomatoes and cook for another 5 minutes, stirring occasionally.
3. Stir in the canned diced tomatoes and tomato paste. Add the vegetable or chicken broth, bay leaf, dried thyme, and dried basil. Season with salt and pepper to taste. Bring to a boil, then reduce the heat and let it simmer for about 20 minutes, or until the tomatoes are tender and flavors are well blended.
4. Remove the bay leaf from the soup.
5. If using, stir in the heavy cream to achieve a creamier texture. Heat through gently, but do not boil after adding the cream.
6. Taste and adjust seasoning if needed.
7. Ladle the hot Provencal Tomato Soup into bowls. Garnish with chopped fresh basil or parsley.
8. Serve hot, optionally topping each serving with croutons for added texture.

Provencal Tomato Soup is perfect as a starter or a light meal, especially when paired with crusty bread or a salad. It's a comforting dish that celebrates the bright and fresh flavors of tomatoes and herbs, characteristic of Provencal cuisine.

Soupe de Lentilles (Lentil Soup)

Ingredients:

- 1 cup dried lentils (green or brown), rinsed and drained
- 2 tablespoons olive oil
- 1 onion, chopped
- 2 cloves garlic, minced
- 2 carrots, diced
- 2 celery stalks, diced
- 1 potato, peeled and diced
- 1 can (14 oz) diced tomatoes
- 6 cups vegetable or chicken broth
- 1 bay leaf
- 1 teaspoon dried thyme
- Salt and pepper to taste
- Fresh parsley, chopped for garnish (optional)
- Lemon wedges for serving (optional)

Instructions:

1. In a large pot, heat olive oil over medium heat. Add the chopped onion and minced garlic. Cook until softened, about 5 minutes.
2. Add the diced carrots, diced celery, and diced potato to the pot. Cook for another 5 minutes, stirring occasionally.
3. Stir in the rinsed lentils and canned diced tomatoes. Add the vegetable or chicken broth, bay leaf, and dried thyme. Season with salt and pepper to taste. Bring to a boil, then reduce the heat and let it simmer for about 30-40 minutes, or until the lentils and vegetables are tender.
4. Taste and adjust seasoning if needed. Remove the bay leaf from the soup.
5. If desired, use an immersion blender to puree a portion of the soup to thicken it, leaving some lentils and vegetables whole for texture.
6. Ladle the hot Lentil Soup into bowls. Garnish with chopped fresh parsley and serve with lemon wedges on the side for squeezing over the soup.

Lentil Soup is a comforting and filling dish that is perfect for colder weather. It's rich in protein and fiber, making it a nutritious option for a satisfying meal. Enjoy it with crusty bread or a side salad for a complete and hearty dinner.

Soupe à la Truffe (Truffle Soup)

Ingredients:

- 1 oz dried or fresh truffles, finely chopped (reserve a few slices for garnish)
- 2 tablespoons butter
- 1 onion, chopped
- 2 cloves garlic, minced
- 2 tablespoons all-purpose flour
- 4 cups chicken or vegetable broth
- 1 cup heavy cream
- Salt and pepper to taste
- Truffle oil (optional, for drizzling)
- Fresh chives or parsley, chopped for garnish

Instructions:

1. In a large pot, melt the butter over medium heat. Add the chopped onion and minced garlic. Cook until softened, about 5 minutes.
2. Stir in the chopped truffles and cook for another 2-3 minutes, allowing the flavors to meld.
3. Sprinkle the flour over the onion and truffle mixture. Stir well to combine and cook for 1-2 minutes to cook out the raw flour taste.
4. Gradually pour in the chicken or vegetable broth, stirring constantly to avoid lumps. Bring to a simmer and cook for about 10-15 minutes, or until the soup thickens slightly.
5. Stir in the heavy cream and season with salt and pepper to taste. Simmer gently for another 5 minutes, stirring occasionally.
6. Remove the soup from heat. If desired, use an immersion blender to puree the soup until smooth. Alternatively, leave it chunky for texture.
7. Ladle the hot Truffle Soup into bowls. Garnish each serving with a few reserved slices of truffle, chopped chives or parsley, and a drizzle of truffle oil if desired.
8. Serve immediately, accompanied by crusty bread or toast points.

Truffle Soup is a decadent treat that showcases the unique and earthy flavor of truffles. It's perfect for special occasions or when you want to indulge in a luxurious soup experience. Enjoy its rich and creamy texture with the aromatic essence of truffles permeating each spoonful.

Soupe à l'oseille (Sorrel Soup)

Ingredients:

- 1 bunch sorrel leaves, washed and chopped (about 4 cups chopped sorrel)
- 2 tablespoons butter
- 1 onion, chopped
- 2 cloves garlic, minced
- 1 potato, peeled and diced
- 4 cups chicken or vegetable broth
- 1 cup heavy cream
- Salt and pepper to taste
- Fresh chives or parsley, chopped for garnish
- Lemon wedges for serving (optional)

Instructions:

1. In a large pot, melt the butter over medium heat. Add the chopped onion and minced garlic. Cook until softened, about 5 minutes.
2. Add the diced potato to the pot and cook for another 5 minutes, stirring occasionally.
3. Stir in the chopped sorrel leaves and cook for 2-3 minutes until wilted.
4. Pour in the chicken or vegetable broth. Bring to a simmer and cook for about 15-20 minutes, or until the potatoes are tender.
5. Remove the soup from heat. Use an immersion blender to puree the soup until smooth.
6. Stir in the heavy cream and season with salt and pepper to taste. Return the soup to low heat and simmer gently for another 5 minutes.
7. Taste and adjust seasoning if needed.
8. Ladle the hot Sorrel Soup into bowls. Garnish each serving with chopped fresh chives or parsley.
9. Serve immediately, optionally accompanied by lemon wedges for squeezing over the soup to enhance the tangy flavor of sorrel.

Sorrel Soup is light, refreshing, and perfect for spring or summer meals. The tartness of sorrel leaves adds a unique and pleasant twist to this creamy soup, making it a delightful addition to your French cuisine repertoire.

Soupe de Pois (Pea Soup)

Ingredients:

- 2 tablespoons butter
- 1 onion, chopped
- 2 cloves garlic, minced
- 4 cups chicken or vegetable broth
- 1 lb frozen peas (about 4 cups)
- 1 potato, peeled and diced
- 1/2 cup heavy cream (optional)
- Salt and pepper to taste
- Fresh mint leaves, chopped for garnish (optional)
- Crème fraîche or yogurt for serving (optional)

Instructions:

1. In a large pot, melt the butter over medium heat. Add the chopped onion and minced garlic. Cook until softened, about 5 minutes.
2. Add the diced potato to the pot and cook for another 5 minutes, stirring occasionally.
3. Pour in the chicken or vegetable broth. Bring to a simmer and cook for about 10 minutes, or until the potatoes are tender.
4. Add the frozen peas to the pot. Simmer for an additional 5-7 minutes, or until the peas are heated through and tender.
5. Remove the soup from heat. Use an immersion blender to puree the soup until smooth. Alternatively, you can transfer the soup in batches to a blender and blend until smooth, then return it to the pot.
6. Stir in the heavy cream, if using, to add richness to the soup. Season with salt and pepper to taste.
7. Return the soup to low heat and simmer gently for another 5 minutes.
8. Ladle the hot Pea Soup into bowls. Garnish each serving with chopped fresh mint leaves, and add a dollop of crème fraîche or yogurt if desired.
9. Serve immediately, accompanied by crusty bread or toast for a comforting meal.

Pea Soup is a vibrant and delicious dish that highlights the natural sweetness of peas. It's perfect for any season and can be enjoyed as a light meal or a starter. The addition of mint leaves and cream enhances its flavor and texture, making it a favorite among soup lovers.

Soupe aux Champignons (Mushroom Soup)

Ingredients:

- 1 lb mushrooms (such as cremini, button, or wild mushrooms), cleaned and sliced
- 2 tablespoons butter
- 1 onion, chopped
- 2 cloves garlic, minced
- 4 cups chicken or vegetable broth
- 1/2 cup dry white wine
- 1 tablespoon all-purpose flour
- 1 cup heavy cream
- Salt and pepper to taste
- Fresh parsley, chopped for garnish
- Croutons or toasted bread for serving (optional)

Instructions:

1. In a large pot, melt the butter over medium heat. Add the chopped onion and minced garlic. Cook until softened, about 5 minutes.
2. Add the sliced mushrooms to the pot. Cook for 8-10 minutes, stirring occasionally, until the mushrooms are tender and browned.
3. Sprinkle the flour over the mushrooms and stir well to combine. Cook for 1-2 minutes to cook out the raw flour taste.
4. Pour in the dry white wine to deglaze the pot, scraping up any browned bits from the bottom. Cook for 2-3 minutes until the wine has reduced slightly.
5. Add the chicken or vegetable broth to the pot. Bring to a simmer and cook for about 15-20 minutes, allowing the flavors to meld together.
6. Stir in the heavy cream and season with salt and pepper to taste. Simmer gently for another 5 minutes.
7. Taste and adjust seasoning if needed.
8. Ladle the hot Mushroom Soup into bowls. Garnish each serving with chopped fresh parsley.
9. Serve immediately, optionally accompanied by croutons or toasted bread for dipping.

Mushroom Soup is a comforting and luxurious dish that is perfect for any occasion. The combination of tender mushrooms, creamy broth, and aromatic herbs creates a delicious and satisfying soup experience. Enjoy it as a starter or as a main dish with your favorite bread on the side.

Soupe de Cresson (Watercress Soup)

Ingredients:

- 2 bunches watercress, washed and tough stems removed
- 2 tablespoons butter
- 1 onion, chopped
- 2 cloves garlic, minced
- 1 potato, peeled and diced
- 4 cups chicken or vegetable broth
- 1/2 cup heavy cream (optional)
- Salt and pepper to taste
- Fresh chives or parsley, chopped for garnish
- Lemon wedges for serving (optional)

Instructions:

1. In a large pot, melt the butter over medium heat. Add the chopped onion and minced garlic. Cook until softened, about 5 minutes.
2. Add the diced potato to the pot and cook for another 5 minutes, stirring occasionally.
3. Pour in the chicken or vegetable broth. Bring to a simmer and cook for about 10 minutes, or until the potatoes are tender.
4. Add the watercress to the pot. Simmer for an additional 5 minutes, or until the watercress is wilted and tender.
5. Remove the soup from heat. Use an immersion blender to puree the soup until smooth. Alternatively, transfer the soup in batches to a blender and blend until smooth, then return it to the pot.
6. Stir in the heavy cream, if using, to add richness to the soup. Season with salt and pepper to taste.
7. Return the soup to low heat and simmer gently for another 5 minutes.
8. Ladle the hot Watercress Soup into bowls. Garnish each serving with chopped fresh chives or parsley.
9. Serve immediately, optionally accompanied by lemon wedges for squeezing over the soup to enhance the flavors.

Watercress Soup is a delightful and nutritious dish that is perfect for a light meal or as a starter. The peppery flavor of watercress shines through in this creamy and comforting soup, making it a favorite among those who appreciate fresh and vibrant flavors in their cuisine.

Soupe de Potiron (Pumpkin Soup)

Ingredients:

- 2 tablespoons butter
- 1 onion, chopped
- 2 cloves garlic, minced
- 1 medium-sized pumpkin (about 4-5 cups diced), peeled, seeded, and diced
- 4 cups vegetable or chicken broth
- 1 cup heavy cream
- 1 teaspoon ground nutmeg
- Salt and pepper to taste
- Fresh parsley or chives, chopped for garnish
- Croutons or toasted bread for serving (optional)

Instructions:

1. In a large pot, melt the butter over medium heat. Add the chopped onion and minced garlic. Cook until softened, about 5 minutes.
2. Add the diced pumpkin to the pot. Cook for another 5-7 minutes, stirring occasionally.
3. Pour in the vegetable or chicken broth. Bring to a simmer and cook for about 15-20 minutes, or until the pumpkin is tender and easily pierced with a fork.
4. Remove the pot from heat. Use an immersion blender to puree the soup until smooth. Alternatively, transfer the soup in batches to a blender and blend until smooth, then return it to the pot.
5. Stir in the heavy cream and ground nutmeg. Season with salt and pepper to taste.
6. Return the soup to low heat and simmer gently for another 5 minutes to heat through.
7. Taste and adjust seasoning if needed.
8. Ladle the hot Pumpkin Soup into bowls. Garnish each serving with chopped fresh parsley or chives.
9. Serve immediately, optionally accompanied by croutons or toasted bread for dipping.

Pumpkin Soup is a comforting and nutritious dish that celebrates the flavors of autumn. The creamy texture and subtle sweetness of pumpkin, combined with warming spices like nutmeg, make it a favorite for cozy meals. Enjoy it as a starter or a light meal, accompanied by crusty bread or a side salad for a satisfying dining experience.

Soupe de Poisson à la Rouille (Fish Soup with Rouille)

Ingredients for the Fish Soup:

- 1 lb white fish fillets (such as cod, haddock, or sea bass), cut into chunks
- 1 lb mixed seafood (such as shrimp, mussels, and/or scallops), cleaned and shelled if needed
- 2 tablespoons olive oil
- 1 onion, chopped
- 2 cloves garlic, minced
- 1 fennel bulb, thinly sliced
- 1 leek, white and light green parts thinly sliced
- 1 carrot, diced
- 1 celery stalk, diced
- 1 tomato, chopped
- 1 tablespoon tomato paste
- 1 cup dry white wine
- 6 cups fish or seafood broth
- 1 bay leaf
- 1 teaspoon dried thyme
- Salt and pepper to taste
- Fresh parsley, chopped for garnish

Ingredients for the Rouille:

- 1/2 cup mayonnaise
- 2 cloves garlic, minced
- 1 teaspoon Dijon mustard
- 1 teaspoon paprika
- Pinch of cayenne pepper (optional)
- 1-2 tablespoons reserved fish soup broth

Instructions:

For the Fish Soup:

1. In a large pot, heat olive oil over medium heat. Add the chopped onion and minced garlic. Cook until softened, about 5 minutes.
2. Add the thinly sliced fennel, sliced leek, diced carrot, and diced celery to the pot. Cook for another 5-7 minutes, stirring occasionally.
3. Stir in the chopped tomato and tomato paste. Cook for 2-3 minutes, stirring constantly.
4. Pour in the dry white wine to deglaze the pot, scraping up any browned bits from the bottom. Cook for 3-4 minutes until the wine has reduced slightly.
5. Add the fish or seafood broth to the pot. Bring to a simmer and add the bay leaf and dried thyme. Season with salt and pepper to taste.
6. Add the chunks of white fish fillets and mixed seafood to the pot. Simmer gently for about 8-10 minutes, or until the seafood is cooked through and opaque.
7. Taste and adjust seasoning if needed. Remove the bay leaf before serving.

For the Rouille:

1. In a small bowl, combine mayonnaise, minced garlic, Dijon mustard, paprika, and cayenne pepper (if using). Mix well to combine.
2. Gradually add 1-2 tablespoons of the reserved fish soup broth to the rouille mixture, stirring continuously, until it reaches a smooth and creamy consistency.

To Serve:

1. Ladle the hot Fish Soup into bowls. Top each serving with a dollop of rouille.
2. Garnish with chopped fresh parsley.
3. Serve immediately, accompanied by crusty bread or garlic bread.

Soupe de Poisson à la Rouille is a hearty and flavorful seafood soup that is perfect for a special occasion or a comforting meal. The rouille adds a creamy and slightly spicy kick to complement the rich flavors of the fish and seafood broth. Enjoy this traditional French dish with friends and family for a memorable dining experience.

Soupe de Carottes (Carrot Soup)

Ingredients:

- 2 tablespoons butter
- 1 onion, chopped
- 2 cloves garlic, minced
- 1 lb carrots, peeled and chopped (about 4-5 cups chopped carrots)
- 4 cups vegetable or chicken broth
- 1 potato, peeled and diced (optional, for added creaminess)
- 1/2 cup heavy cream (optional)
- Salt and pepper to taste
- Fresh parsley or chives, chopped for garnish
- Croutons or toasted bread for serving (optional)

Instructions:

1. In a large pot, melt the butter over medium heat. Add the chopped onion and minced garlic. Cook until softened, about 5 minutes.
2. Add the chopped carrots to the pot. Cook for another 5-7 minutes, stirring occasionally.
3. Pour in the vegetable or chicken broth. If using, add the diced potato for added creaminess. Bring to a simmer and cook for about 15-20 minutes, or until the carrots (and potato, if using) are tender and easily pierced with a fork.
4. Remove the pot from heat. Use an immersion blender to puree the soup until smooth. Alternatively, transfer the soup in batches to a blender and blend until smooth, then return it to the pot.
5. Stir in the heavy cream, if using, to add richness to the soup. Season with salt and pepper to taste.
6. Return the soup to low heat and simmer gently for another 5 minutes to heat through.
7. Taste and adjust seasoning if needed.
8. Ladle the hot Carrot Soup into bowls. Garnish each serving with chopped fresh parsley or chives.
9. Serve immediately, optionally accompanied by croutons or toasted bread for dipping.

Carrot Soup is a nutritious and comforting dish that is perfect for any time of year. The sweetness of carrots combined with the creamy texture makes it a favorite among soup lovers. Enjoy it as a starter or as a light meal, paired with your favorite bread for a satisfying dining experience.

Soupe de Navet (Turnip Soup)

Ingredients:

- 2 tablespoons butter
- 1 onion, chopped
- 2 cloves garlic, minced
- 2-3 large turnips, peeled and diced (about 4-5 cups diced turnips)
- 1 potato, peeled and diced (optional, for added creaminess)
- 4 cups vegetable or chicken broth
- 1 bay leaf
- 1 teaspoon dried thyme
- Salt and pepper to taste
- 1/2 cup heavy cream (optional)
- Fresh parsley, chopped for garnish
- Croutons or toasted bread for serving (optional)

Instructions:

1. In a large pot, melt the butter over medium heat. Add the chopped onion and minced garlic. Cook until softened, about 5 minutes.
2. Add the diced turnips (and potato, if using) to the pot. Cook for another 5-7 minutes, stirring occasionally.
3. Pour in the vegetable or chicken broth. Add the bay leaf and dried thyme. Bring to a simmer and cook for about 15-20 minutes, or until the turnips (and potato, if using) are tender and easily pierced with a fork.
4. Remove the bay leaf from the pot. Use an immersion blender to puree the soup until smooth. Alternatively, transfer the soup in batches to a blender and blend until smooth, then return it to the pot.
5. Stir in the heavy cream, if using, to add richness to the soup. Season with salt and pepper to taste.
6. Return the soup to low heat and simmer gently for another 5 minutes to heat through.
7. Taste and adjust seasoning if needed.
8. Ladle the hot Turnip Soup into bowls. Garnish each serving with chopped fresh parsley.
9. Serve immediately, optionally accompanied by croutons or toasted bread for dipping.

Turnip Soup is a comforting and nutritious dish that is perfect for colder months. The earthy flavor of turnips combined with the creamy texture makes it a satisfying meal. Enjoy it as a starter or as a light meal, paired with crusty bread for a complete dining experience.

Soupe à la Bière (Beer Soup)

Ingredients:

- 2 tablespoons butter
- 1 onion, finely chopped
- 2 cloves garlic, minced
- 2 carrots, diced
- 2 celery stalks, diced
- 2 potatoes, peeled and diced
- 4 cups chicken or vegetable broth
- 1 bottle (12 oz) of your favorite beer (choose a flavorful beer like ale or lager)
- 1 tablespoon all-purpose flour
- 1 cup heavy cream
- Salt and pepper to taste
- Fresh parsley, chopped for garnish
- Croutons or toasted bread for serving (optional)

Instructions:

1. In a large pot, melt the butter over medium heat. Add the finely chopped onion and minced garlic. Cook until softened, about 5 minutes.
2. Add the diced carrots, diced celery, and diced potatoes to the pot. Cook for another 5-7 minutes, stirring occasionally.
3. Sprinkle the flour over the vegetables and stir well to coat. Cook for 1-2 minutes to cook out the raw flour taste.
4. Gradually pour in the chicken or vegetable broth, stirring constantly to avoid lumps. Bring to a simmer and cook for about 15 minutes, or until the vegetables are tender.
5. Stir in the beer and bring the soup back to a simmer. Cook for an additional 5 minutes to allow the flavors to meld together.
6. Stir in the heavy cream and season with salt and pepper to taste. Simmer gently for another 5 minutes.
7. Taste and adjust seasoning if needed.
8. Ladle the hot Beer Soup into bowls. Garnish each serving with chopped fresh parsley.
9. Serve immediately, optionally accompanied by croutons or toasted bread for dipping.

Beer Soup is a hearty and warming dish that is perfect for cooler weather. The combination of beer, vegetables, and cream creates a rich and flavorful soup that is sure to satisfy. Enjoy it as a starter or as a main dish with your favorite crusty bread on the side.

Soupe à la Fane de Radis (Radish Green Soup)

Ingredients:

- Greens from 1 bunch of radishes, washed and roughly chopped
- 2 tablespoons butter
- 1 onion, chopped
- 2 cloves garlic, minced
- 1 potato, peeled and diced
- 4 cups vegetable or chicken broth
- 1/2 cup heavy cream (optional)
- Salt and pepper to taste
- Fresh parsley or chives, chopped for garnish
- Croutons or toasted bread for serving (optional)

Instructions:

1. In a large pot, melt the butter over medium heat. Add the chopped onion and minced garlic. Cook until softened, about 5 minutes.
2. Add the diced potato to the pot. Cook for another 5 minutes, stirring occasionally.
3. Pour in the vegetable or chicken broth. Bring to a simmer and cook for about 10 minutes, or until the potatoes are tender.
4. Add the chopped radish greens to the pot. Simmer for an additional 5-7 minutes, or until the greens are wilted and tender.
5. Remove the pot from heat. Use an immersion blender to puree the soup until smooth. Alternatively, transfer the soup in batches to a blender and blend until smooth, then return it to the pot.
6. Stir in the heavy cream, if using, to add richness to the soup. Season with salt and pepper to taste.
7. Return the soup to low heat and simmer gently for another 5 minutes to heat through.
8. Taste and adjust seasoning if needed.
9. Ladle the hot Radish Green Soup into bowls. Garnish each serving with chopped fresh parsley or chives.
10. Serve immediately, optionally accompanied by croutons or toasted bread for dipping.

Radish Green Soup is a flavorful and nutritious way to use every part of the radish plant. The greens impart a fresh and slightly peppery taste to the soup, making it a unique addition to your soup repertoire. Enjoy it as a starter or a light meal, paired with your favorite bread for a satisfying dining experience.

Soupe aux Légumes (Vegetable Soup)

Ingredients:

- 2 tablespoons olive oil
- 1 onion, chopped
- 2 cloves garlic, minced
- 2 carrots, diced
- 2 celery stalks, diced
- 1 potato, peeled and diced
- 1 zucchini, diced
- 1 cup green beans, chopped
- 1 tomato, chopped (or 1 cup canned diced tomatoes)
- 6 cups vegetable or chicken broth
- 1 bay leaf
- 1 teaspoon dried thyme
- Salt and pepper to taste
- Fresh parsley or basil, chopped for garnish
- Croutons or toasted bread for serving (optional)

Instructions:

1. In a large pot, heat the olive oil over medium heat. Add the chopped onion and minced garlic. Cook until softened, about 5 minutes.
2. Add the diced carrots, diced celery, diced potato, diced zucchini, chopped green beans, and chopped tomato to the pot. Cook for another 5-7 minutes, stirring occasionally.
3. Pour in the vegetable or chicken broth. Add the bay leaf and dried thyme. Bring to a simmer and cook for about 15-20 minutes, or until the vegetables are tender.
4. Remove the bay leaf from the pot. Season with salt and pepper to taste.
5. Taste and adjust seasoning if needed.
6. Ladle the hot Vegetable Soup into bowls. Garnish each serving with chopped fresh parsley or basil.
7. Serve immediately, optionally accompanied by croutons or toasted bread for dipping.

Vegetable Soup is a comforting and nutritious dish that can be customized with your favorite vegetables. It's perfect for any season and can be enjoyed as a starter or a light meal. The combination of fresh vegetables and savory broth makes it a wholesome and satisfying option for lunch or dinner.

Soupe aux Poireaux (Leek Soup)

Ingredients:

- 3 leeks, white and light green parts only, cleaned and thinly sliced
- 2 tablespoons butter
- 1 onion, chopped
- 2 cloves garlic, minced
- 1 potato, peeled and diced
- 4 cups vegetable or chicken broth
- 1 bay leaf
- 1 teaspoon dried thyme
- 1/2 cup heavy cream (optional)
- Salt and pepper to taste
- Fresh chives or parsley, chopped for garnish
- Croutons or toasted bread for serving (optional)

Instructions:

1. In a large pot, melt the butter over medium heat. Add the chopped onion and minced garlic. Cook until softened, about 5 minutes.
2. Add the thinly sliced leeks to the pot. Cook for another 5-7 minutes, stirring occasionally, until the leeks are softened.
3. Add the diced potato to the pot. Cook for 5 minutes, stirring occasionally.
4. Pour in the vegetable or chicken broth. Add the bay leaf and dried thyme. Bring to a simmer and cook for about 15-20 minutes, or until the potatoes are tender.
5. Remove the bay leaf from the pot. Use an immersion blender to puree the soup until smooth. Alternatively, transfer the soup in batches to a blender and blend until smooth, then return it to the pot.
6. Stir in the heavy cream, if using, to add richness to the soup. Season with salt and pepper to taste.
7. Return the soup to low heat and simmer gently for another 5 minutes to heat through.
8. Taste and adjust seasoning if needed.
9. Ladle the hot Leek Soup into bowls. Garnish each serving with chopped fresh chives or parsley.
10. Serve immediately, optionally accompanied by croutons or toasted bread for dipping.

Leek Soup is a comforting and creamy soup that is perfect for cooler weather. The mild and slightly sweet flavor of leeks combined with the creamy texture makes it a favorite among soup lovers. Enjoy it as a starter or as a light meal, paired with crusty bread for a satisfying dining experience.

Soupe à la Châtaigne (Chestnut Soup)

Ingredients:

- 1 lb fresh chestnuts, or 2 cups peeled and cooked chestnuts (canned or vacuum-packed)
- 2 tablespoons butter
- 1 onion, chopped
- 2 cloves garlic, minced
- 1 celery stalk, chopped
- 1 carrot, chopped
- 4 cups vegetable or chicken broth
- 1 bay leaf
- 1 teaspoon dried thyme
- 1/2 cup heavy cream
- Salt and pepper to taste
- Fresh parsley or chives, chopped for garnish
- Croutons or toasted bread for serving (optional)

Instructions:

1. If using fresh chestnuts, start by making a small slit on the flat side of each chestnut with a sharp knife. Place the chestnuts in a pot of boiling water and cook for about 15 minutes. Drain and let them cool slightly, then peel off the outer shell and inner skin. Chop the chestnuts coarsely.
2. In a large pot, melt the butter over medium heat. Add the chopped onion, minced garlic, chopped celery, and chopped carrot. Cook until softened, about 5-7 minutes.
3. Add the chopped chestnuts to the pot. Stir and cook for another 2-3 minutes.
4. Pour in the vegetable or chicken broth. Add the bay leaf and dried thyme. Bring to a simmer and cook for about 20-25 minutes, or until the vegetables and chestnuts are tender.
5. Remove the bay leaf from the pot. Use an immersion blender to puree the soup until smooth. Alternatively, transfer the soup in batches to a blender and blend until smooth, then return it to the pot.
6. Stir in the heavy cream to add richness to the soup. Season with salt and pepper to taste.
7. Return the soup to low heat and simmer gently for another 5 minutes to heat through.
8. Taste and adjust seasoning if needed.
9. Ladle the hot Chestnut Soup into bowls. Garnish each serving with chopped fresh parsley or chives.
10. Serve immediately, optionally accompanied by croutons or toasted bread for dipping.

Chestnut Soup is a luxurious and comforting dish that is perfect for autumn and winter. The nutty flavor of chestnuts combined with the creamy texture makes it a delightful treat for soup enthusiasts. Enjoy it as a starter or as a light meal, paired with your favorite bread for a satisfying dining experience.

Soupe aux Moules (Mussel Soup)

Ingredients:

- 2 lbs fresh mussels, cleaned and debearded
- 2 tablespoons butter
- 1 onion, finely chopped
- 2 cloves garlic, minced
- 1 leek, white and light green parts thinly sliced
- 1 carrot, diced
- 1 celery stalk, diced
- 1 tomato, chopped
- 1/2 cup dry white wine
- 4 cups fish or seafood broth
- 1 bay leaf
- 1 teaspoon dried thyme
- Salt and pepper to taste
- 1/2 cup heavy cream (optional)
- Fresh parsley, chopped for garnish
- Crusty bread for serving

Instructions:

1. In a large pot, melt the butter over medium heat. Add the chopped onion, minced garlic, thinly sliced leek, diced carrot, and diced celery. Cook until softened, about 5-7 minutes.
2. Add the chopped tomato to the pot. Cook for another 2-3 minutes, stirring occasionally.
3. Pour in the dry white wine to deglaze the pot, scraping up any browned bits from the bottom. Cook for 3-4 minutes until the wine has reduced slightly.
4. Add the fish or seafood broth to the pot. Bring to a simmer.
5. Add the bay leaf and dried thyme to the pot. Season with salt and pepper to taste.
6. Add the cleaned mussels to the pot. Cover and cook for about 5-7 minutes, or until the mussels have opened. Discard any mussels that do not open.
7. Remove the pot from heat. Use a slotted spoon to transfer the mussels to a bowl, leaving the broth in the pot. Remove and discard the bay leaf.
8. Use an immersion blender to puree the broth until smooth. Alternatively, transfer the broth in batches to a blender and blend until smooth, then return it to the pot.
9. Stir in the heavy cream, if using, to add richness to the soup.
10. Return the pot to low heat and simmer gently for another 5 minutes to heat through.
11. Taste and adjust seasoning if needed.
12. To serve, ladle the hot Mussel Soup into bowls. Arrange the cooked mussels in their shells on top of the soup. Garnish with chopped fresh parsley.
13. Serve immediately, accompanied by crusty bread for dipping into the flavorful broth.

Mussel Soup is a flavorful and elegant dish that makes a perfect starter for a special meal. The combination of fresh mussels, aromatic vegetables, and creamy broth creates a delightful dining experience that is sure to impress. Enjoy this soup with family and friends for a taste of French coastal cuisine at home.

Soupe de Céleri-rave (Celery Root Soup)

Ingredients:

- 1 celery root (céleri-rave), peeled and diced (about 4 cups diced celery root)
- 2 tablespoons butter
- 1 onion, chopped
- 2 cloves garlic, minced
- 1 potato, peeled and diced
- 4 cups vegetable or chicken broth
- 1 bay leaf
- 1 teaspoon dried thyme
- 1/2 cup heavy cream
- Salt and pepper to taste
- Fresh parsley or chives, chopped for garnish
- Croutons or toasted bread for serving (optional)

Instructions:

1. In a large pot, melt the butter over medium heat. Add the chopped onion and minced garlic. Cook until softened, about 5 minutes.
2. Add the diced celery root and diced potato to the pot. Cook for another 5-7 minutes, stirring occasionally.
3. Pour in the vegetable or chicken broth. Add the bay leaf and dried thyme. Bring to a simmer and cook for about 15-20 minutes, or until the celery root and potato are tender.
4. Remove the bay leaf from the pot. Use an immersion blender to puree the soup until smooth. Alternatively, transfer the soup in batches to a blender and blend until smooth, then return it to the pot.
5. Stir in the heavy cream to add richness to the soup. Season with salt and pepper to taste.
6. Return the soup to low heat and simmer gently for another 5 minutes to heat through.
7. Taste and adjust seasoning if needed.
8. Ladle the hot Celery Root Soup into bowls. Garnish each serving with chopped fresh parsley or chives.
9. Serve immediately, optionally accompanied by croutons or toasted bread for dipping.

Celery Root Soup is a comforting and flavorful dish that is perfect for colder months. The subtle and earthy flavor of celery root combined with the creamy texture makes it a satisfying meal. Enjoy it as a starter or as a light meal, paired with your favorite bread for a complete dining experience.

Soupe de Maïs (Corn Soup)

Ingredients:

- 4 cups fresh corn kernels (from about 4-5 ears of corn) or frozen corn
- 2 tablespoons butter
- 1 onion, chopped
- 2 cloves garlic, minced
- 1 potato, peeled and diced
- 4 cups vegetable or chicken broth
- 1 bay leaf
- 1 teaspoon dried thyme
- 1/2 cup heavy cream
- Salt and pepper to taste
- Fresh chives or parsley, chopped for garnish
- Croutons or toasted bread for serving (optional)

Instructions:

1. If using fresh corn, shuck the corn and remove the kernels from the cobs. Set aside.
2. In a large pot, melt the butter over medium heat. Add the chopped onion and minced garlic. Cook until softened, about 5 minutes.
3. Add the diced potato to the pot. Cook for another 5 minutes, stirring occasionally.
4. Add the corn kernels to the pot. Cook for 3-4 minutes, stirring occasionally.
5. Pour in the vegetable or chicken broth. Add the bay leaf and dried thyme. Bring to a simmer and cook for about 15-20 minutes, or until the potatoes are tender.
6. Remove the bay leaf from the pot. Use an immersion blender to puree the soup until smooth. Alternatively, transfer the soup in batches to a blender and blend until smooth, then return it to the pot.
7. Stir in the heavy cream to add richness to the soup. Season with salt and pepper to taste.
8. Return the soup to low heat and simmer gently for another 5 minutes to heat through.
9. Taste and adjust seasoning if needed.
10. Ladle the hot Corn Soup into bowls. Garnish each serving with chopped fresh chives or parsley.
11. Serve immediately, optionally accompanied by croutons or toasted bread for dipping.

Corn Soup is a comforting and flavorful dish that is perfect for summer or any time of the year when corn is in season. The natural sweetness of corn combined with the creamy texture makes it a satisfying and delicious meal. Enjoy it as a starter or as a light meal, paired with crusty bread for a complete dining experience.

Soupe aux Asperges (Asparagus Soup)

Ingredients:

- 1 lb asparagus, tough ends trimmed and cut into 1-inch pieces
- 2 tablespoons butter
- 1 onion, chopped
- 2 cloves garlic, minced
- 1 potato, peeled and diced
- 4 cups vegetable or chicken broth
- 1 bay leaf
- 1 teaspoon dried thyme
- 1/2 cup heavy cream
- Salt and pepper to taste
- Fresh chives or parsley, chopped for garnish
- Croutons or toasted bread for serving (optional)

Instructions:

1. In a large pot, melt the butter over medium heat. Add the chopped onion and minced garlic. Cook until softened, about 5 minutes.
2. Add the diced potato to the pot. Cook for another 5 minutes, stirring occasionally.
3. Add the asparagus pieces to the pot. Cook for 3-4 minutes, stirring occasionally.
4. Pour in the vegetable or chicken broth. Add the bay leaf and dried thyme. Bring to a simmer and cook for about 15-20 minutes, or until the potatoes and asparagus are tender.
5. Remove the bay leaf from the pot. Use an immersion blender to puree the soup until smooth. Alternatively, transfer the soup in batches to a blender and blend until smooth, then return it to the pot.
6. Stir in the heavy cream to add richness to the soup. Season with salt and pepper to taste.
7. Return the soup to low heat and simmer gently for another 5 minutes to heat through.
8. Taste and adjust seasoning if needed.
9. Ladle the hot Asparagus Soup into bowls. Garnish each serving with chopped fresh chives or parsley.
10. Serve immediately, optionally accompanied by croutons or toasted bread for dipping.

Asparagus Soup is a light and refreshing dish that is perfect for spring when asparagus is in season. The delicate flavor of asparagus combined with the creamy texture makes it a delightful starter or a light meal. Enjoy it with crusty bread or a side salad for a complete dining experience.

Soupe au Cresson (Watercress Soup)

Ingredients:

- 4 cups fresh watercress, tough stems removed
- 2 tablespoons butter
- 1 onion, chopped
- 2 cloves garlic, minced
- 1 potato, peeled and diced
- 4 cups vegetable or chicken broth
- 1 bay leaf
- 1 teaspoon dried thyme
- 1/2 cup heavy cream
- Salt and pepper to taste
- Fresh chives or parsley, chopped for garnish
- Croutons or toasted bread for serving (optional)

Instructions:

1. In a large pot, melt the butter over medium heat. Add the chopped onion and minced garlic. Cook until softened, about 5 minutes.
2. Add the diced potato to the pot. Cook for another 5 minutes, stirring occasionally.
3. Add the fresh watercress to the pot. Cook for 2-3 minutes, stirring occasionally, until wilted.
4. Pour in the vegetable or chicken broth. Add the bay leaf and dried thyme. Bring to a simmer and cook for about 15-20 minutes, or until the potatoes are tender.
5. Remove the bay leaf from the pot. Use an immersion blender to puree the soup until smooth. Alternatively, transfer the soup in batches to a blender and blend until smooth, then return it to the pot.
6. Stir in the heavy cream to add richness to the soup. Season with salt and pepper to taste.
7. Return the soup to low heat and simmer gently for another 5 minutes to heat through.
8. Taste and adjust seasoning if needed.
9. Ladle the hot Watercress Soup into bowls. Garnish each serving with chopped fresh chives or parsley.
10. Serve immediately, optionally accompanied by croutons or toasted bread for dipping.

Watercress Soup is a light and refreshing dish that is perfect for any time of the year. The peppery flavor of watercress combined with the creamy texture makes it a delightful starter or a light meal. Enjoy it with crusty bread or a side salad for a complete dining experience.

Soupe au Vin Blanc (White Wine Soup)

Ingredients:

- 2 tablespoons butter
- 1 onion, chopped
- 2 cloves garlic, minced
- 1 leek, white and light green parts thinly sliced
- 1 carrot, diced
- 1 celery stalk, diced
- 1 potato, peeled and diced
- 4 cups vegetable or chicken broth
- 1 bay leaf
- 1 teaspoon dried thyme
- 1/2 cup dry white wine
- 1/2 cup heavy cream
- Salt and pepper to taste
- Fresh parsley, chopped for garnish
- Croutons or toasted bread for serving (optional)

Instructions:

1. In a large pot, melt the butter over medium heat. Add the chopped onion, minced garlic, sliced leek, diced carrot, and diced celery. Cook until softened, about 5-7 minutes.
2. Add the diced potato to the pot. Cook for another 5 minutes, stirring occasionally.
3. Pour in the dry white wine to deglaze the pot, scraping up any browned bits from the bottom. Cook for 3-4 minutes until the wine has reduced slightly.
4. Add the vegetable or chicken broth to the pot. Add the bay leaf and dried thyme. Bring to a simmer and cook for about 15-20 minutes, or until the vegetables are tender.
5. Remove the bay leaf from the pot. Use an immersion blender to puree the soup until smooth. Alternatively, transfer the soup in batches to a blender and blend until smooth, then return it to the pot.
6. Stir in the heavy cream to add richness to the soup. Season with salt and pepper to taste.
7. Return the soup to low heat and simmer gently for another 5 minutes to heat through.
8. Taste and adjust seasoning if needed.
9. Ladle the hot soup into bowls. Garnish each serving with chopped fresh parsley.
10. Serve immediately, optionally accompanied by croutons or toasted bread for dipping.

This adaptation incorporates white wine into a creamy vegetable soup, offering a rich and flavorful option that showcases the influence of wine in French cuisine. Adjust the ingredients and seasonings according to your taste preferences, and enjoy this soup as a delightful starter or light meal.

Soupe aux Poissons et aux Crustacés (Seafood Soup)

Ingredients:

- 1 lb mixed seafood (such as shrimp, scallops, mussels, and firm white fish like cod or halibut), cleaned and prepared
- 2 tablespoons olive oil
- 1 onion, chopped
- 2 cloves garlic, minced
- 1 fennel bulb, thinly sliced
- 1 leek, white and light green parts thinly sliced
- 1 carrot, diced
- 1 celery stalk, diced
- 1 tomato, chopped
- 1/2 cup dry white wine
- 4 cups fish or seafood broth
- 1 bay leaf
- 1 teaspoon dried thyme
- 1/2 cup heavy cream (optional)
- Salt and pepper to taste
- Fresh parsley, chopped for garnish
- Crusty bread for serving

Instructions:

1. In a large pot, heat the olive oil over medium heat. Add the chopped onion, minced garlic, thinly sliced fennel, sliced leek, diced carrot, and diced celery. Cook until softened, about 5-7 minutes.
2. Add the chopped tomato to the pot. Cook for another 2-3 minutes, stirring occasionally.
3. Pour in the dry white wine to deglaze the pot, scraping up any browned bits from the bottom. Cook for 3-4 minutes until the wine has reduced slightly.
4. Add the fish or seafood broth to the pot. Add the bay leaf and dried thyme. Bring to a simmer and cook for about 15-20 minutes, or until the vegetables are tender.
5. Meanwhile, prepare the seafood: if using mussels, scrub and debeard them. If using shrimp, peel and devein them. Cut the firm white fish into bite-sized pieces.
6. Add the mixed seafood to the pot. Cook for 5-7 minutes, or until the seafood is cooked through and mussels have opened. Discard any mussels that do not open.
7. Remove the bay leaf from the pot. Stir in the heavy cream, if using, to add richness to the soup. Season with salt and pepper to taste.
8. Taste and adjust seasoning if needed.
9. Ladle the hot Seafood Soup into bowls. Garnish each serving with chopped fresh parsley.
10. Serve immediately, accompanied by crusty bread for dipping into the flavorful broth.

Seafood Soup is a luxurious and satisfying dish that is perfect for seafood lovers. The combination of fresh seafood, aromatic vegetables, and creamy broth creates a delightful dining experience reminiscent of coastal French cuisine. Enjoy it as a starter or as a light meal, paired with a glass of white wine for an authentic French dining experience.

Soupe de Patates Douces (Sweet Potato Soup)

Ingredients:

- 2 tablespoons olive oil
- 1 onion, chopped
- 2 cloves garlic, minced
- 2 lbs sweet potatoes, peeled and diced
- 1 carrot, diced
- 1 celery stalk, diced
- 4 cups vegetable or chicken broth
- 1 bay leaf
- 1 teaspoon dried thyme
- 1/2 teaspoon ground cinnamon
- Pinch of nutmeg
- 1/2 cup coconut milk (optional, for creaminess)
- Salt and pepper to taste
- Fresh cilantro or parsley, chopped for garnish
- Croutons or toasted bread for serving (optional)

Instructions:

1. In a large pot, heat the olive oil over medium heat. Add the chopped onion and minced garlic. Cook until softened, about 5 minutes.
2. Add the diced sweet potatoes, carrot, and celery to the pot. Cook for another 5 minutes, stirring occasionally.
3. Pour in the vegetable or chicken broth. Add the bay leaf, dried thyme, ground cinnamon, and nutmeg. Bring to a simmer and cook for about 15-20 minutes, or until the sweet potatoes and vegetables are tender.
4. Remove the bay leaf from the pot. Use an immersion blender to puree the soup until smooth. Alternatively, transfer the soup in batches to a blender and blend until smooth, then return it to the pot.
5. Stir in the coconut milk, if using, to add creaminess to the soup. Season with salt and pepper to taste.
6. Return the soup to low heat and simmer gently for another 5 minutes to heat through.
7. Taste and adjust seasoning if needed.
8. Ladle the hot Sweet Potato Soup into bowls. Garnish each serving with chopped fresh cilantro or parsley.
9. Serve immediately, optionally accompanied by croutons or toasted bread for dipping.

Sweet Potato Soup is a comforting and nutritious dish that is perfect for cooler days. The natural sweetness of sweet potatoes combined with aromatic spices creates a warm and satisfying soup that the whole family will enjoy. Serve it as a starter or as a light meal, paired with crusty bread for a complete dining experience.

Soupe aux Choux (Cabbage Soup)

Ingredients:

- 2 tablespoons olive oil
- 1 onion, chopped
- 2 cloves garlic, minced
- 1 small head of green cabbage, shredded
- 2 carrots, peeled and diced
- 2 potatoes, peeled and diced
- 4 cups vegetable or chicken broth
- 1 bay leaf
- 1 teaspoon dried thyme
- Salt and pepper to taste
- Fresh parsley, chopped for garnish
- Crusty bread for serving

Instructions:

1. In a large pot, heat the olive oil over medium heat. Add the chopped onion and minced garlic. Cook until softened, about 5 minutes.
2. Add the shredded cabbage, diced carrots, and diced potatoes to the pot. Cook for another 5 minutes, stirring occasionally.
3. Pour in the vegetable or chicken broth. Add the bay leaf and dried thyme. Bring to a simmer and cook for about 20-25 minutes, or until the vegetables are tender.
4. Remove the bay leaf from the pot. Season the soup with salt and pepper to taste.
5. Ladle the hot Cabbage Soup into bowls. Garnish each serving with chopped fresh parsley.
6. Serve immediately, accompanied by crusty bread for dipping into the flavorful broth.

Cabbage Soup is a comforting and nutritious dish that is perfect for colder days. The combination of tender cabbage, hearty vegetables, and aromatic herbs creates a delicious and satisfying soup that warms both body and soul. Enjoy it as a starter or as a light meal, paired with your favorite bread for a complete dining experience.

Soupe aux Poireaux et Pommes de Terre (Potato Leek Soup)

Ingredients:

- 2 tablespoons butter
- 2 leeks, white and light green parts thinly sliced
- 2 cloves garlic, minced
- 3 large potatoes, peeled and diced
- 4 cups vegetable or chicken broth
- 1 bay leaf
- 1 teaspoon dried thyme
- 1/2 cup heavy cream (optional, for added richness)
- Salt and pepper to taste
- Fresh chives or parsley, chopped for garnish
- Croutons or toasted bread for serving (optional)

Instructions:

1. In a large pot, melt the butter over medium heat. Add the sliced leeks and minced garlic. Cook until softened, about 5-7 minutes.
2. Add the diced potatoes to the pot. Cook for another 5 minutes, stirring occasionally.
3. Pour in the vegetable or chicken broth. Add the bay leaf and dried thyme. Bring to a simmer and cook for about 15-20 minutes, or until the potatoes are tender.
4. Remove the bay leaf from the pot. Use an immersion blender to puree the soup until smooth. Alternatively, transfer the soup in batches to a blender and blend until smooth, then return it to the pot.
5. Stir in the heavy cream, if using, to add richness to the soup. Season with salt and pepper to taste.
6. Return the soup to low heat and simmer gently for another 5 minutes to heat through.
7. Taste and adjust seasoning if needed.
8. Ladle the hot Potato Leek Soup into bowls. Garnish each serving with chopped fresh chives or parsley.
9. Serve immediately, optionally accompanied by croutons or toasted bread for dipping.

Potato Leek Soup is a comforting and hearty dish that is perfect for colder days. The combination of tender potatoes, aromatic leeks, and creamy broth creates a delicious and satisfying soup that is enjoyed across French cuisine. Serve it as a starter or as a light meal, paired with crusty bread for a complete dining experience.

Soupe de Salsifis (Salsify Soup)

Ingredients:

- 1 lb salsify roots
- 2 tablespoons butter
- 1 onion, chopped
- 2 cloves garlic, minced
- 1 potato, peeled and diced
- 4 cups vegetable or chicken broth
- 1 bay leaf
- 1 teaspoon dried thyme
- 1/2 cup heavy cream
- Salt and pepper to taste
- Fresh parsley, chopped for garnish
- Croutons or toasted bread for serving (optional)

Instructions:

1. Peel the salsify roots using a vegetable peeler. Cut them into small pieces and immediately place them in a bowl of cold water with a splash of vinegar to prevent browning.
2. In a large pot, melt the butter over medium heat. Add the chopped onion and minced garlic. Cook until softened, about 5-7 minutes.
3. Drain the salsify pieces and add them to the pot along with the diced potato. Cook for another 5 minutes, stirring occasionally.
4. Pour in the vegetable or chicken broth. Add the bay leaf and dried thyme. Bring to a simmer and cook for about 20-25 minutes, or until the salsify and potato are tender.
5. Remove the bay leaf from the pot. Use an immersion blender to puree the soup until smooth. Alternatively, transfer the soup in batches to a blender and blend until smooth, then return it to the pot.
6. Stir in the heavy cream to add richness to the soup. Season with salt and pepper to taste.
7. Return the soup to low heat and simmer gently for another 5 minutes to heat through.
8. Taste and adjust seasoning if needed.
9. Ladle the hot Salsify Soup into bowls. Garnish each serving with chopped fresh parsley.
10. Serve immediately, optionally accompanied by croutons or toasted bread for dipping.

Salsify Soup is a unique and flavorful dish that showcases the delicate taste of salsify. Enjoy it as a starter or a light meal, paired with crusty bread for a complete dining experience that highlights the root vegetable's distinct flavor.

Soupe au Pistou (Vegetable Soup with Pesto)

Ingredients:

For the Soup:

- 2 tablespoons olive oil
- 1 onion, chopped
- 2 cloves garlic, minced
- 2 carrots, diced
- 2 celery stalks, diced
- 2 zucchini, diced
- 1 potato, peeled and diced
- 1 can (14 oz) diced tomatoes
- 6 cups vegetable or chicken broth
- 1 bay leaf
- 1 teaspoon dried thyme
- Salt and pepper to taste
- 1 cup small pasta (such as ditalini or small shells)

For the Pistou:

- 2 cups fresh basil leaves
- 2 cloves garlic, minced
- 1/4 cup grated Parmesan cheese
- 1/4 cup pine nuts or walnuts
- 1/2 cup olive oil
- Salt and pepper to taste

Instructions:

1. **Make the Soup:**
   - In a large pot, heat olive oil over medium heat. Add chopped onion and minced garlic. Cook until softened, about 5 minutes.
   - Add diced carrots, celery, zucchini, and potato to the pot. Cook for another 5 minutes, stirring occasionally.
   - Stir in diced tomatoes, vegetable or chicken broth, bay leaf, and dried thyme. Bring to a simmer and cook for about 15-20 minutes, or until vegetables are tender.
   - Season with salt and pepper to taste.
   - Add small pasta to the soup and cook according to package instructions until al dente. Remove from heat.
2. **Make the Pistou:**
   - In a food processor or blender, combine fresh basil leaves, minced garlic, grated Parmesan cheese, and pine nuts or walnuts.
   - Pulse until ingredients are finely chopped.
   - With the motor running, slowly drizzle in olive oil until mixture forms a smooth paste.
   - Season with salt and pepper to taste.
3. **Serve:**
   - Ladle the hot Vegetable Soup into bowls.

- Top each serving with a generous spoonful of Pistou.
- Optionally, garnish with additional grated Parmesan cheese and fresh basil leaves.
- Serve immediately, accompanied by crusty bread for a satisfying meal.

Soupe au Pistou is a hearty and flavorful soup that is perfect for showcasing fresh summer vegetables. The addition of Pistou adds a burst of basil and garlic flavor, making it a delightful and comforting dish for any occasion. Enjoy this soup as a main course or as a starter to a Provencal-inspired meal.

Soupe de Champignons Sauvages (Wild Mushroom Soup)

Ingredients:

- 1 lb wild mushrooms (such as porcini, chanterelles, or morels), cleaned and sliced
- 2 tablespoons butter
- 1 onion, chopped
- 2 cloves garlic, minced
- 1 potato, peeled and diced
- 4 cups vegetable or chicken broth
- 1 bay leaf
- 1 teaspoon dried thyme
- 1/2 cup heavy cream
- Salt and pepper to taste
- Fresh parsley, chopped for garnish
- Truffle oil (optional, for drizzling)
- Crusty bread for serving

Instructions:

1. In a large pot, melt the butter over medium heat. Add the chopped onion and minced garlic. Cook until softened, about 5 minutes.
2. Add the sliced wild mushrooms to the pot. Cook for another 5-7 minutes, stirring occasionally, until mushrooms release their liquid and begin to brown.
3. Add the diced potato to the pot. Cook for another 2-3 minutes, stirring occasionally.
4. Pour in the vegetable or chicken broth. Add the bay leaf and dried thyme. Bring to a simmer and cook for about 15-20 minutes, or until the mushrooms and potatoes are tender.
5. Remove the bay leaf from the pot. Use an immersion blender to puree the soup until smooth. Alternatively, transfer the soup in batches to a blender and blend until smooth, then return it to the pot.
6. Stir in the heavy cream to add richness to the soup. Season with salt and pepper to taste.
7. Return the soup to low heat and simmer gently for another 5 minutes to heat through.
8. Taste and adjust seasoning if needed.
9. Ladle the hot Wild Mushroom Soup into bowls. Garnish each serving with chopped fresh parsley and a drizzle of truffle oil, if desired.
10. Serve immediately, accompanied by crusty bread for dipping into the flavorful broth.

Wild Mushroom Soup is a luxurious and comforting dish that highlights the earthy flavors of wild mushrooms. Enjoy it as a starter or as a light meal, paired with a glass of white wine for an elegant dining experience that celebrates the rich bounty of mushrooms.

Soupe aux Fruits de Mer (Seafood Soup)

Ingredients:

- 1 lb mixed seafood (such as shrimp, scallops, mussels, and firm white fish like cod or halibut), cleaned and prepared
- 2 tablespoons olive oil
- 1 onion, chopped
- 2 cloves garlic, minced
- 1 fennel bulb, thinly sliced
- 1 leek, white and light green parts thinly sliced
- 1 carrot, diced
- 1 celery stalk, diced
- 1 tomato, chopped
- 1/2 cup dry white wine
- 4 cups fish or seafood broth
- 1 bay leaf
- 1 teaspoon dried thyme
- 1/2 cup heavy cream (optional, for added richness)
- Salt and pepper to taste
- Fresh parsley, chopped for garnish
- Crusty bread for serving

Instructions:

1. In a large pot, heat the olive oil over medium heat. Add the chopped onion, minced garlic, thinly sliced fennel, sliced leek, diced carrot, and diced celery. Cook until softened, about 5-7 minutes.
2. Add the chopped tomato to the pot. Cook for another 2-3 minutes, stirring occasionally.
3. Pour in the dry white wine to deglaze the pot, scraping up any browned bits from the bottom. Cook for 3-4 minutes until the wine has reduced slightly.
4. Add the fish or seafood broth to the pot. Add the bay leaf and dried thyme. Bring to a simmer and cook for about 15-20 minutes, or until the vegetables are tender.
5. Meanwhile, prepare the seafood: if using mussels, scrub and debeard them. If using shrimp, peel and devein them. Cut the firm white fish into bite-sized pieces.
6. Add the mixed seafood to the pot. Cook for 5-7 minutes, or until the seafood is cooked through and mussels have opened. Discard any mussels that do not open.
7. Remove the bay leaf from the pot. Stir in the heavy cream, if using, to add richness to the soup. Season with salt and pepper to taste.
8. Taste and adjust seasoning if needed.
9. Ladle the hot Seafood Soup into bowls. Garnish each serving with chopped fresh parsley.
10. Serve immediately, accompanied by crusty bread for dipping into the flavorful broth.

Soupe aux Fruits de Mer is a delightful and hearty soup that is perfect for seafood lovers. The combination of fresh seafood, aromatic vegetables, and creamy broth creates a satisfying dish that is ideal as a starter or as a main course. Enjoy it with a glass of chilled white wine for a complete French-inspired dining experience.

Soupe aux Topinambours (Jerusalem Artichoke Soup)

Ingredients:

- 1 lb Jerusalem artichokes (also known as sunchokes), peeled and diced
- 2 tablespoons butter
- 1 onion, chopped
- 2 cloves garlic, minced
- 1 potato, peeled and diced
- 4 cups vegetable or chicken broth
- 1 bay leaf
- 1 teaspoon dried thyme
- 1/2 cup heavy cream
- Salt and pepper to taste
- Fresh chives or parsley, chopped for garnish
- Croutons or toasted bread for serving (optional)

Instructions:

1. In a large pot, melt the butter over medium heat. Add the chopped onion and minced garlic. Cook until softened, about 5 minutes.
2. Add the diced Jerusalem artichokes and potato to the pot. Cook for another 5 minutes, stirring occasionally.
3. Pour in the vegetable or chicken broth. Add the bay leaf and dried thyme. Bring to a simmer and cook for about 20-25 minutes, or until the Jerusalem artichokes and potato are tender.
4. Remove the bay leaf from the pot. Use an immersion blender to puree the soup until smooth. Alternatively, transfer the soup in batches to a blender and blend until smooth, then return it to the pot.
5. Stir in the heavy cream to add richness to the soup. Season with salt and pepper to taste.
6. Return the soup to low heat and simmer gently for another 5 minutes to heat through.
7. Taste and adjust seasoning if needed.
8. Ladle the hot Jerusalem Artichoke Soup into bowls. Garnish each serving with chopped fresh chives or parsley.
9. Serve immediately, optionally accompanied by croutons or toasted bread for dipping.

Jerusalem Artichoke Soup is a creamy and flavorful dish that highlights the nutty and slightly sweet taste of Jerusalem artichokes. Enjoy it as a starter or as a light meal, paired with your favorite bread for a delicious and comforting dining experience.

Soupe à l'Estragon (Tarragon Soup)

Ingredients:

- 2 tablespoons butter
- 1 onion, chopped
- 2 cloves garlic, minced
- 4 cups chicken or vegetable broth
- 1 potato, peeled and diced
- 1 carrot, peeled and diced
- 1 celery stalk, diced
- 1/2 cup fresh tarragon leaves, chopped
- 1 bay leaf
- Salt and pepper to taste
- 1/2 cup heavy cream
- Fresh tarragon leaves, for garnish

Instructions:

1. In a large pot, melt the butter over medium heat. Add the chopped onion and minced garlic. Cook until softened, about 5 minutes.
2. Add the diced potato, carrot, and celery to the pot. Cook for another 5 minutes, stirring occasionally.
3. Pour in the chicken or vegetable broth. Add the bay leaf and chopped tarragon leaves (reserve some for garnish). Bring to a simmer and cook for about 15-20 minutes, or until the vegetables are tender.
4. Remove the bay leaf from the pot. Use an immersion blender to puree the soup until smooth. Alternatively, transfer the soup in batches to a blender and blend until smooth, then return it to the pot.
5. Stir in the heavy cream to add richness to the soup. Season with salt and pepper to taste.
6. Return the soup to low heat and simmer gently for another 5 minutes to heat through.
7. Taste and adjust seasoning if needed.
8. Ladle the hot Tarragon Soup into bowls. Garnish each serving with a few fresh tarragon leaves.
9. Serve immediately, accompanied by crusty bread or a light salad for a delightful meal.

Soupe à l'Estragon is a refreshing and aromatic soup that is perfect for showcasing the delicate flavor of tarragon. Enjoy it as a starter or as a light meal, paired with your favorite side dishes for a complete and satisfying dining experience.

Soupe de Poulet aux Vermicelles (Chicken Noodle Soup)

Ingredients:

- 1 tablespoon olive oil
- 1 onion, finely chopped
- 2 carrots, peeled and diced
- 2 celery stalks, diced
- 2 cloves garlic, minced
- 1 teaspoon dried thyme
- 1 bay leaf
- 6 cups chicken broth
- 2 cups cooked chicken, shredded or diced
- 1 cup vermicelli noodles (or any small pasta)
- Salt and pepper to taste
- Fresh parsley, chopped for garnish (optional)
- Lemon wedges for serving (optional)

Instructions:

1. In a large pot, heat the olive oil over medium heat. Add the chopped onion, diced carrots, and diced celery. Cook until softened, about 5-7 minutes.
2. Add the minced garlic, dried thyme, and bay leaf to the pot. Cook for another minute until fragrant.
3. Pour in the chicken broth and bring to a simmer. Cook for about 10 minutes to allow the flavors to meld.
4. Add the cooked chicken to the pot. If using uncooked chicken, add it earlier and cook until it's fully cooked through.
5. Stir in the vermicelli noodles (or other small pasta) and cook according to package instructions until tender.
6. Season the soup with salt and pepper to taste.
7. Remove the bay leaf from the pot.
8. Ladle the hot Chicken Noodle Soup into bowls. Garnish each serving with chopped fresh parsley, if desired.
9. Serve immediately, optionally with a squeeze of lemon juice for added freshness.

Chicken Noodle Soup is a comforting and nourishing dish that's perfect for chilly days or when you need a warm, satisfying meal. Enjoy it as a starter or a complete meal on its own, paired with crusty bread for dipping into the flavorful broth.

Soupe à la Tomate (Tomato Soup)

Ingredients:

- 2 tablespoons olive oil
- 1 onion, chopped
- 2 cloves garlic, minced
- 1 carrot, peeled and diced
- 1 celery stalk, diced
- 2 lbs ripe tomatoes, chopped (or 2 cans of diced tomatoes)
- 4 cups vegetable or chicken broth
- 1 bay leaf
- 1 teaspoon dried thyme
- Salt and pepper to taste
- 1/2 cup heavy cream (optional, for added richness)
- Fresh basil leaves, chopped, for garnish
- Croutons or toasted bread for serving (optional)

Instructions:

1. In a large pot, heat olive oil over medium heat. Add chopped onion and minced garlic. Cook until softened, about 5 minutes.
2. Add diced carrot and celery to the pot. Cook for another 5 minutes, stirring occasionally.
3. Add chopped tomatoes to the pot (if using fresh tomatoes, you can peel them beforehand by blanching in boiling water for 1 minute, then plunging into ice water and peeling). Cook for 10 minutes, stirring occasionally, until tomatoes start to break down.
4. Pour in vegetable or chicken broth. Add bay leaf and dried thyme. Bring to a simmer and cook for 15-20 minutes, or until vegetables are tender.
5. Remove bay leaf from the pot. Use an immersion blender to puree the soup until smooth. Alternatively, carefully transfer soup in batches to a blender and blend until smooth, then return to the pot.
6. Stir in heavy cream, if using, to add richness to the soup. Season with salt and pepper to taste.
7. Return soup to low heat and simmer gently for another 5 minutes to heat through.
8. Taste and adjust seasoning if needed.
9. Ladle hot Tomato Soup into bowls. Garnish each serving with chopped fresh basil leaves.
10. Serve immediately, optionally with croutons or toasted bread for dipping.

Tomato Soup is a classic favorite that's perfect as a starter or a comforting meal on its own. Enjoy its rich flavors and smooth texture, served hot for a satisfying and heartwarming experience.

Soupe aux Légumes Verts (Green Vegetable Soup)

Ingredients:

- 2 tablespoons olive oil
- 1 onion, chopped
- 2 cloves garlic, minced
- 2 cups green beans, trimmed and cut into pieces
- 2 cups fresh spinach leaves
- 2 cups broccoli florets
- 1 zucchini, diced
- 4 cups vegetable or chicken broth
- 1 bay leaf
- 1 teaspoon dried thyme
- Salt and pepper to taste
- 1/2 cup heavy cream (optional, for added richness)
- Fresh parsley or basil leaves, chopped, for garnish

Instructions:

1. In a large pot, heat olive oil over medium heat. Add chopped onion and minced garlic. Cook until softened, about 5 minutes.
2. Add green beans, spinach, broccoli florets, and diced zucchini to the pot. Cook for another 5 minutes, stirring occasionally.
3. Pour in vegetable or chicken broth. Add bay leaf and dried thyme. Bring to a simmer and cook for 15-20 minutes, or until vegetables are tender.
4. Remove bay leaf from the pot. Use an immersion blender to puree the soup until smooth. Alternatively, carefully transfer soup in batches to a blender and blend until smooth, then return to the pot.
5. Stir in heavy cream, if using, to add richness to the soup. Season with salt and pepper to taste.
6. Return soup to low heat and simmer gently for another 5 minutes to heat through.
7. Taste and adjust seasoning if needed.
8. Ladle hot Green Vegetable Soup into bowls. Garnish each serving with chopped fresh parsley or basil leaves.
9. Serve immediately, optionally with crusty bread or a side salad for a complete meal.

This Green Vegetable Soup is vibrant, nutritious, and perfect for showcasing the flavors of fresh green vegetables. Enjoy it as a light lunch or dinner, and savor the goodness of seasonal greens in every spoonful.

Soupe de Poireaux et Pommes de Terre (Leek and Potato Soup)

Ingredients:

- 2 tablespoons butter
- 2 leeks, white and light green parts only, sliced
- 2 potatoes, peeled and diced
- 4 cups vegetable or chicken broth
- 1 bay leaf
- Salt and pepper to taste
- 1/2 cup heavy cream (optional, for added richness)
- Fresh chives or parsley, chopped, for garnish

Instructions:

1. In a large pot, melt the butter over medium heat. Add the sliced leeks and cook, stirring occasionally, until softened, about 5-7 minutes.
2. Add the diced potatoes to the pot. Cook for another 5 minutes, stirring occasionally.
3. Pour in the vegetable or chicken broth. Add the bay leaf. Bring to a simmer and cook for about 15-20 minutes, or until the potatoes are tender.
4. Remove the bay leaf from the pot. Use an immersion blender to puree the soup until smooth. Alternatively, carefully transfer the soup in batches to a blender and blend until smooth, then return it to the pot.
5. Stir in the heavy cream, if using, to add richness to the soup. Season with salt and pepper to taste.
6. Return the soup to low heat and simmer gently for another 5 minutes to heat through.
7. Taste and adjust seasoning if needed.
8. Ladle the hot Leek and Potato Soup into bowls. Garnish each serving with chopped fresh chives or parsley.
9. Serve immediately, optionally with crusty bread or a side salad for a complete meal.

This Leek and Potato Soup is comforting and satisfying, perfect for chilly days or whenever you crave a creamy and flavorful soup. Enjoy its simplicity and rich taste, ideal as a starter or a light main dish.

Soupe à l'Orange (Orange Soup)

Ingredients:

- 2 tablespoons butter
- 1 onion, finely chopped
- 2 cloves garlic, minced
- 4 large oranges, juiced (about 2 cups fresh orange juice)
- Zest of 1 orange
- 4 cups vegetable or chicken broth
- 1 teaspoon ground cumin
- 1/2 teaspoon ground coriander
- Salt and pepper to taste
- 1/2 cup heavy cream (optional, for added richness)
- Fresh cilantro or parsley, chopped, for garnish

Instructions:

1. In a large pot, melt the butter over medium heat. Add the chopped onion and minced garlic. Cook until softened, about 5 minutes.
2. Add the ground cumin and ground coriander to the pot. Stir and cook for another minute until fragrant.
3. Pour in the fresh orange juice and vegetable or chicken broth. Add the orange zest. Bring to a simmer and cook for about 15 minutes to allow flavors to meld.
4. Remove the pot from heat. Use an immersion blender to puree the soup until smooth. Alternatively, carefully transfer the soup in batches to a blender and blend until smooth, then return it to the pot.
5. Stir in the heavy cream, if using, to add richness to the soup. Season with salt and pepper to taste.
6. Return the soup to low heat and simmer gently for another 5 minutes to heat through.
7. Taste and adjust seasoning if needed.
8. Ladle the hot Orange Soup into bowls. Garnish each serving with chopped fresh cilantro or parsley.
9. Serve immediately, optionally with a slice of crusty bread or a light salad on the side.

Soupe à l'Orange is a refreshing and surprising soup that can be enjoyed as a starter or a unique addition to your soup repertoire. Its vibrant citrus flavors combined with aromatic spices create a memorable dish that's perfect for brightening up any meal.

Soupe de Poireaux et Pommes de Terre (Leek and Potato Soup)

Ingredients:

- 2 tablespoons butter
- 2 leeks, white and light green parts only, thinly sliced
- 2 potatoes, peeled and diced
- 4 cups vegetable or chicken broth
- 1 bay leaf
- Salt and pepper, to taste
- 1/2 cup heavy cream (optional, for added richness)
- Fresh chives or parsley, chopped, for garnish

Instructions:

1. In a large pot, melt the butter over medium heat.
2. Add the sliced leeks and cook, stirring occasionally, until softened, about 5-7 minutes.
3. Add the diced potatoes to the pot and stir to combine with the leeks.
4. Pour in the vegetable or chicken broth and add the bay leaf.
5. Bring the mixture to a boil, then reduce the heat to low and simmer for about 20-25 minutes, or until the potatoes are tender.
6. Remove the bay leaf from the pot.
7. Using an immersion blender, blend the soup until smooth and creamy. If you don't have an immersion blender, carefully transfer the soup in batches to a blender and blend until smooth, then return it to the pot.
8. Stir in the heavy cream, if using, and season with salt and pepper to taste.
9. Simmer the soup for an additional 5 minutes to heat through and allow the flavors to meld.
10. Ladle the soup into bowls and garnish with chopped fresh chives or parsley.
11. Serve hot, optionally with a slice of crusty bread or a side salad.

This Leek and Potato Soup is creamy, comforting, and perfect for any occasion. Enjoy its rich flavors and smooth texture as a starter or a light meal.

Soupe à l'Estragon

Ingredients:

- 2 tablespoons butter
- 1 onion, finely chopped
- 2 cloves garlic, minced
- 4 cups chicken or vegetable broth
- 1 potato, peeled and diced
- 1 carrot, peeled and diced
- 1 celery stalk, diced
- 1/2 cup fresh tarragon leaves, chopped
- 1 bay leaf
- Salt and pepper, to taste
- 1/2 cup heavy cream (optional, for added richness)
- Fresh tarragon leaves, chopped, for garnish

Instructions:

1. In a large pot, melt the butter over medium heat.
2. Add the chopped onion and minced garlic. Cook until softened, about 5 minutes.
3. Add the diced potato, carrot, and celery to the pot. Cook for another 5 minutes, stirring occasionally.
4. Pour in the chicken or vegetable broth. Add the bay leaf and chopped tarragon leaves (reserve some for garnish). Bring to a simmer and cook for about 20 minutes, or until the vegetables are tender.
5. Remove the bay leaf from the pot.
6. Use an immersion blender to puree the soup until smooth. Alternatively, carefully transfer the soup in batches to a blender and blend until smooth, then return it to the pot.
7. Stir in the heavy cream, if using, to add richness to the soup. Season with salt and pepper to taste.
8. Simmer the soup for an additional 5 minutes to heat through and allow the flavors to meld.
9. Taste and adjust seasoning if needed.
10. Ladle the hot Tarragon Soup into bowls. Garnish each serving with chopped fresh tarragon leaves.
11. Serve immediately, optionally with a slice of crusty bread or a side salad.

This Soupe à l'Estragon is fragrant, creamy, and showcases the unique taste of tarragon. Enjoy it as a comforting starter or a light meal, and savor its delicate flavors.

www.ingramcontent.com/pod-product-compliance
Lightning Source LLC
LaVergne TN
LVHW081322060526
838201LV00055B/2405